T0196444

Something to Chew On

Something to Chew On

Digesting Healthy Spiritual Food for the Soul in the Calendar Year Ahead

ARI JOSHUA BOUSE

iUniverse®

SOMETHING TO CHEW ON
Digesting Healthy Spiritual Food for the Soul in the Calendar Year Ahead

iUniverse books may be ordered through booksellers or by contacting:

iUniverse
1663 Liberty Drive
Bloomington, IN 47403
www.iuniverse.com
1-800-Authors (1-800-288-4677)

Because of the dynamic nature of the Internet, any web addresses or links contained in this book may have changed since publication and may no longer be valid. The views expressed in this work are solely those of the author and do not necessarily reflect the views of the publisher, and the publisher hereby disclaims any responsibility for them.

Any people depicted in stock imagery provided by Thinkstock are models, and such images are being used for illustrative purposes only.
Certain stock imagery © Thinkstock.

ISBN: 978-1-4917-9606-1 (sc)
ISBN: 978-1-4917-9607-8 (e)

Library of Congress Control Number: 2016907194

Print information available on the last page.

iUniverse rev. date: 05/13/2016

Introduction

How Did This Book Come About?

Shortly after my mom died of suicide back in 1995, I was in a dark place and full of pain and suffering. But I also felt an incredible surge of energy and a rebirth in my being. Not long thereafter, my aunt Barbara and I felt inspired to collaborate on a project together combining my prose with her art and began discussing this idea further. She had just completed a master's degree in art therapy, while I was working on my master's degree in social work. Since that time, we have been living our lives separated by time and space but connected in spirit. During that continuum, we have revisited this conversation every now and again. However, for a long time our idea remained a bit of a pipe dream. Although it has been a process, an animal-spirit-calendar idea to capture nature's seasonal energy has evolved into this chapter book of guided meditations. Each month is inspired by the consciousness of an animal-spirit guide to function as spiritual power for living in a new age and paradigm. The intention of this book is to help all of us breathe in fresh air into our souls. In that process, may we then exhale the dead air of old ways that no longer serve us so we are equipped to live authentically.

I use the terms *animal spirits*, *power animals*, *animal totems*, and *spirit guides* interchangeably. On the other hand, I do respect and appreciate that some disciplines clearly differentiate these terms and energies. Do you remember when ancestral wisdom recognized that animals have been here a lot longer than we have? As such, shamanic ancestors were inspired by their apparent capacity to harmonize with the natural environment and ascribed a spiritual power to this observation. When humanity landed on the playing field, we came to see our animal friends as helpers to develop a kindred relationship with the natural world. There is so much help available to us from the spirit realm, if only we humble ourselves to ask for it and allow ourselves to receive. When we bow to the wisdom of the natural world, we bring a deeper knowing of harmony and balance into our souls and waking lives. In this way, we get to know our souls on a deeper level. Given that we incarnated as souls in human bodies, we are awakening to the understanding that we are spiritual beings having human experiences. We recognize that we are travelers here in spirit-mind-body vessels. As such, we need to consume an energetic diet that nourishes our souls so we can become the change we want to see in the world. I look at this as soulful program development. And we are designing a new program.

Bringing the Energy of Inner Peace into Our Daily Experience with Meditation

Inner peace is like a calm ocean deep within your being and is accessed and known through meditation. I define *meditation* as an experiential state of consciousness that is experienced by sustaining awareness. Meditation is a space of being present in a way that we aware that we are aware. But in reality, it is a label-, thought-, and judgment-free zone. Energy medicine is both spiritual and scientific in nature. As such, we humans are part of that nature, and we are prewired for spirituality. Meditation on animal spirits is a powerful energetic diet for us to consume in our daily lives. I hope you will see this book as a travel guide while tracking your own trails and blazing your own path. The illustrations that accompany the prose are designed to help you integrate a picture of the animal spirit into your mind and soul. Commitment to this discipline will collectively help us take our next evolutionary step as earthlings to live in harmony with our deeply mysterious universe. If anything, meditation helps us sit with what is, no matter how challenging or uncomfortable. Remember that the Chinese symbol for crisis and opportunity is the same. I see this as a recognition of paradox, opposite sides of the same coin, and the tension of opposites that are always with us. How do we make friends with that?

I remember learning that the best laboratory to study the scientific method is in the naturalistic environment. Out on the trails, so to speak, is where we collect our anecdotal and experiential spiritual data for authentic living within this classroom known as earth. In our fieldwork, we directly observe that we are living in amazing times here, as climate change is literally unfolding before our eyes. While an old world is dying, a new world is budding in our flowering collective consciousness. Our modern world skates on the thin ice of materialism and mechanistic probabilities that has programmed a hellish nightmare. Moreover, we are moving beyond exclusively experiencing reality in our heads as fixed ideas, intellectual concepts, and fleeting cursory glances, filing away what we see in conceptual file cabinets and reacting to repetitive mental tapes. We are experiencing a great spiritual awakening. There is powerful medicine in learning to merely sit with what is. Sitting with what is through self-reflection is the key to opening new pathways toward experiencing new realities. This is how we cocreate heaven on earth.

We are learning to balance our heads with our hearts—looking through a lens of our souls. In this new age and paradigm, we are moving closer toward the universal power of love and truth. At the same time, we are moving away from the propagated illusion of separation and accompanying suffering. We are waking up from a long sleepwalk. What was once hidden beneath the shadows of our conscious minds is now rising to the surface. What lies below the tip of the iceberg is becoming clearer in our field of vision. When our heads and our hearts dance together, our souls converge in harmony on the ground and in spirit. We are becoming high-minded and also growing deep roots into Mother Earth.

When peering into the realm of infinity, we see possibilities and solutions revealed. Here we see our challenges, but more importantly, we recognize and focus on opportunities. There is death and rebirth in every waking moment. We are healing our polarity by integrating our internal masculine and feminine energies. In this way, we are bringing balance to ourselves. Instead of divisive, ego-driven us-and-them segregations, judging ourselves and one another as either superior or inferior, we sit in circles and see that all voices are truly valued. In this space, we know oneness and celebrate the good times of our diversity within our unity. We welcome win-win scenarios for all of us to share through giving and receiving. This is not easy, as it takes a conscious intention to choose to see a silver lining and focus on the positive. But we are not speaking of a fictitious utopian (or dystopian) ideal or fantasy. Rather, we are speaking of a subjective experience and unfolding process. The more of us allow for that, the more it becomes us living our new dream together.

On channel now, it is time for us to become present with ourselves. Now is the time to relax and let go of our egotism, dramas, pretending, and getting lost in our distractions that serve as roadblocks to being present. Paying careful attention to the cyclical way of nature helps us stay in alignment with the flow of Spirit's universal energy. One powerful and yet simple strategy for embodying this process is getting outdoors, connecting with our animal friends, and heeding the cadence of their spirited wisdom by taking sound field notes. Mother Nature is a gift that keeps on giving, regardless of what the seasonal harvest yields.

How to Access the Animal-Spirit Guides through the Meditative Journeying Process

Here is one possible shamanic journey that I would like to share with you. As I understand it, the journey process is about shifting our experience from our conscious or ordinary experience with reality, to an experience with the alternate, extraordinary realities. This is both a spiritual and scientific process, as our perceptions and brain waves change form. Thus, a shift in our state of consciousness occurs when we journey and meditate. We journey to ask the spirit realm for help to become more conscious and aware during our living experience with material reality.

A Simple Method for Journeying

- Light incense/candle.
- Clear your mind and calm down.
- Relax your gaze, with your eyes almost crossed/vision slightly blurred, and meditate on a specific animal in your book.
- Start drumming or rattling to a consistent beat in your sacred space.
- Let yourself perceive the animal's energy in your consciousness, and allow it to enter into your being.
- Ask the animal spirit for guidance, let go, and then notice wherever it takes you during your journey. Observe any sounds, thoughts, words, visuals, and the like, that come up.
- Be sure to thank the animal for any information that it shared with you.
- Before returning to this reality, it is important to change the drum beat for an effective transition. This is called a call back. (For example, after ten to twenty minutes of drumming, I open my eyes and then hit the drum eight times for three repetitions, then three times for three repetitions, and then seven times for three repetitions to signal the end of my journey. But your call back can be in the form of a word, a thought, or a mantra that works for you.)
- Record what comes up for you during your journey.

About the Author

Ari Joshua Bouse is a licensed clinical social worker and Reiki master who incorporates meditation and shamanism into his mystical way of living. Ari is an embodiment of the possibility of overcoming deep soul wounds and an inspirational role model to the reality of inner peace. Ari is passionate about breathing in a mental health perspective in public schools and helping children develop good social skills for effective living. He lives with his wife, their child, and a garden variety of animal friends. If you would like to reach Ari, please feel free to contact him via e-mail at: darknightwalksinsunlight@gmail.com or check out his website at www.classroommothershipearth.wordpress.com.

About the Artist

Barbara Merlotti is a visual artist, production designer for film, and ballroom dancer. Raised in the Midwest, she attended the Museum School of Fine Arts, Boston, and Tufts University in the 1980s. In the next decade, she returned to the Midwest and eventually earned an MFA in art therapy in 1994, and in the early 2000s, a received a BFA in art education. She currently lives with her husband, two dogs, and a cat on a farm in Missouri.

Acknowledgment

I would like to thank God and the spirit realm for all Your love, guidance, and support. Thank You for coming through living creatures and nature so we can incorporate powerful spiritual politics for living in this reality. It is from a deep place of radical humility that I bow to the wonders of a shamanistic worldview, Taoist energetic perspective, and all those that have been instrumental in reawakening its ancient indigenous wisdom to the modern Western reality. I feel great joy in witnessing a convergence of scientific and spiritual harmony at this time. May this book of guided meditations inspire a renewed sense of adventure and synchronicity in your own life and its ripple effect on others.

Chapter 1

Becoming the Moon with Wolf in January

Wolf guides us along the trails to balance our own unique tracks with our kindred pack connection …

Do you remember when hungry wolf packs howled outside old tribal villages?

Humans, like wolves, have a strong orientation of rugged individualism—coupled with a strong sense of pack family kinship.

A passing winter solstice reveals an exit strategy for many souls that leave behind earth at this junction …

But their imprint lives on …

Wolves embody a delicate balance of authentic soul expression with respect for the pack mentality.

Our key connections to the moon unlock hidden knowledge and wisdom.

What is lurking beneath your conscious experience with reality?

Let wolf awaken your own wise teacher within.

May we learn to sit with life's unfolding mystery.

Contemplate your experiences with anger for a moment …

Are you feeding your inner wise wolf or the angry wolf?

Feel the fire of a wolf's heartbeat …

Picture a wolf to fully become the moon.

Lay the tracks of change you want to see in your field of vision.

Lighten up your energy field to see positive and constructive pathways ahead

Commentary

Anger is a primal emotion that is an integral part of being human. Some of us do not go any further than our anger—constantly reacting to the ways of the world without reserve. Intimidation, aggression, and even violence are a way of life. And it is easy to stop at justifying our anger by looking at someone or something else as the target of our problem. But the wolf can guide us into the deeper, hidden dens of our souls. Meditation is a process learning to self-reflect. Our emotions are part of being human. We are here to learn how to effectively integrate our emotions into our lives for authentic living. We still have a long way to go. But take a look at the civil rights movement and remember how apartheid was driven out of American culture. Wolf government is inspiring to our developing new world because it is a complex hybrid of a hierarchical and socially democratic culture. Within this balanced system is a carefully woven tapestry of novelty, structure, consistency, and predictability. By feeding the wise wolf teachings, we can learn to transform the energy of our anger and use it to take constructive action. Perhaps you get involved in politics to stand up for social justice.

Or you could start meditating every day to lead the sea of change by starting with yourself. It will have a ripple effect that will help heal the whole wide world and beyond. We are not victims to the dictates of the universe. Rather, we are the universe. And it is here to serve us as we serve it. Let the wolf show you the way.

Chapter 2

Taking It Slow and Low
with Turtle in February

Running a hurried up offense is a popular way to live on earth today ...

Might as well wise up to the turtle's wisdom to remember Mother Earth's ancient wisdom to slow down our tempo and anchor in her ground.

Do you need to escape from the worries of the world for a spell?

Or do you need to come out of your shell and be more social?

Meditate on turtle for a deeper understanding of patience and planetary connection.

A Chinese-Lunar New Year reminds us that spring is arriving energetically, in spite of probable peaks in snowfall accumulation ...

Do you feel the seeds underground starting to think about waking up?

It's time to bury your ideas in the ground and let the sunlight do its business ... so that they may organically blossom in the spring.

Turtle's age-old shell symbolizes soulful protection.

In these hard times … may we weather climate change with mindful wisdom.

Commentary

Turtles are older than dinosaurs and carry an ancient wisdom on their backs. If there are any spirit guides to help us open up to the idea of karma, the turtle is a good role model. Karma can easily be understood as the law of cause and effect. If you are paying attention to the big picture, you start noticing how cause and effect impacts your life and then have ability to transcend it. Have you ever noticed that the more you hurry or try to expedite a process, the more your hurried pace slows you down in the long run? Through patience and compassion, we become equipped to harmonize with our conflicts. Tai chi is often practiced in slow motion. The idea behind this slow and meditative internal martial art is that if you practice it at a slow pace, you will be fast if and when the situation calls for fast action. We slow down, observe the moments as they come without judgment, and learn to be with what is. May we cultivate energy gradually and powerfully like water.

Chapter 3

Diving into Our Soul Potential with Whale in March

With whale, we dive into archives of our planetary consciousness.

Their energy breathes an air of discovery into waters of our soul purpose during our swim here on Mother Earth.

Meditation on the whale invites us to hear the universal heartbeat of Mother Earth's oceanic sea of consciousness.

Spring equinox blossoms a fleeting energetic balance of light and dark …

We move into a time when feminine yin begins to wane as masculine yang waxes on.

Sunlight climbs to its summit on the summer solstice, arriving in later June in the Northern Hemisphere.

The converse is true to our friends in the Southern Hemisphere.

It is their autumn equinox there.

Light and dark energies are equal, but their darkness grows in power, climaxing on their winter solstice, where the darkest day of the year precipitates a slow resurrection of light.

A full worm moon brings the arrival of the robin, signifying that spring has sprung.

Our ancestors identified this full moon as the last of winter.

What better medicine to remedy March madness?

Whales are dedicated to their family.

Their sonar is akin to an acute form of empathy.

In the sense that we can learn to listen in and hear subtle stirrings inside with relationship to self and others, this process increases our sensitivity.

Drinking in deep and relaxed belly breathing is what's on tap for a clear walking meditation.

May we all be spring-fed lakes that leave behind clean water for others to follow in our wake

Commentary

Equinoxes are a good time to reflect on getting in touch with our masculine and feminine energies that coexist within our own selves and our planet. In much the same way as our planet has hemispheres, so do our brains. We are living in a time where we need to wake up to balance by dismantling, healing, and unifying the illusion of separation. The sun does not dominate the moon. Rather they both do their part to sustain homeostasis. Nor does male need to subjugate female. Without the creative energy of feminine power, none of us would be here. Energetic equanimity will help us transition more gracefully into an era of a cocreative, we consciousness. Instead of a divisive us-and-them mentality, we can move deeper into a time when we realize that we all need to work together as uniquely diverse expressions of divine oneness. We need to embrace the tension of opposites and relax into that in our modern world. Yin and yang are always in flux, and nature reflects that to us. Spiritually, the energy of the whale represents an awakening of our soul purpose. March is a time of seasonal transition between the winter and spring. Ideally, we are more introspective and inward during the darker months of winter. But when spring arrives, our budding inner work may blossom outward in a more yang-oriented and external fashion.

Chapter 4

April Hops in with Frog

Here we are hopping further along into spring …

Frog showers us with purifying songs of April rains.

We branch out of a wintery coffin after a soulful, energetic spring cleaning.

Rainbows reflect colorful flowers blossoming with clean care.

A full pink moon reflects an early arrival spring flowers spreading outside.

Abundance and fertility are in the air!

Time to clear away the internal clutter …

Are you remembering to take deep, cleansing breaths to stay grounded?

Might as well transform the way we hop through life and call on the positive vibrations to reverberate in our souls' acoustics

Metamorphosis abounds as May flowers whisper in the winds of change.

Frog awakens magical elemental forces of water and land.

What needs to be released from your mind-body-spirit?

Picture a frog to help you develop a deeper respect for boundaries.

Visualize transformative travels through powerful conductors of water and sound

Your creative powers want to spring forth!

Now is the time to let go of stale, stuck energies that want to uproot your soul's impetus to evolve and grow.

Commentary

Showers in April are a good reminder that it is time to clean up—time for cleansing, purification, detoxification, and release. Nature reflects our inner world for us to examine. The beauty of a rainbow could not exist without the storm that preceded it. And it is often after we feel lost and alone when we suddenly see the rainbow brighten our spirits. Otherwise, we would not be able to differentiate a dark sky from a clear day.

Chapter 5

Swan Paddles in Gracefully into May

May we swim with the grace of a swan as we navigate the flow of energies streaming into these uncharted streams of new age consciousness.

Climate change is upon us … might as well go with the flow rather than trying to push against the current.

A full flower moon awakens our senses to the fragrant floral abundance, cross-pollinating across an awakening new world.

Paddling along with the grace of a swan, might we become inspired?

Let us appreciate the beauty of everyday living, both indoors and outdoors.

Do you see the beauty within your own being and the world around you?

Paradoxically, try to see opportunities for transformation within your transgressions.

Might we dig deep enough to rise up to both the challenge and opportunity to become friends with whatever we do not like about ourselves.

Trying to lead a perfect life is a receipt for unhappiness.

What could you adjust inside yourself when perceiving something outside of yourself as undesirable?

In this space, we open up to the sacred realm of inner peace.

Transient distractions to sitting with what is are conveniently inconvenient pathways away from the now.

Otherwise, cosmetic changes only temporarily placate the little ego.

Commentary

Many times we do not have control over what happens to us in life. But we do have control over the way we respond to what life throws at us. We always have the choice to resist the events that unfold in front of our eyes. Or we can choose to accept and even embrace what comes our way and roll with it as gracefully as possible. Some folks really don't learn to live until they realize they are dying. Still others who have lived on this planet for many years merely exist, hardly more than robotic walking corpses. Energy is energy—it's what you do with it that counts.

Chapter 6

Taking Flight with Butterfly in June

Flitting away from spring, we feel the ripple effect of the rising sunlight peaking on the summer solstice to illuminate our way.

A full strawberry moon celebrates this sweet season for harvesting strawberries.

The light of masculine-yang is at its energetic peak on the summer solstice.

It's time to break out, expand, and drink in the festivities of summertime.

In the Southern Hemisphere, the dark nights of feminine-yin energies are climaxing.

Southern lights start slowly waxing.

Might as well float through the season with the joy of butterfly, spread the spiritual seeds of love for all to enjoy.

Becoming a future self in the here and now, we are creating ourselves anew.

Butterfly's position in our ecosystem gets us to reflect on the their effect on our waking up to the realm of possibility ...

Summer is a good time to nurture outward growth and become a bit of a social butterfly.

We all need to breathe through these trying times ... breathe out the force of fear, breathe in the power of love.

Butterfly is opening up our hearts to smile!

Remember to be gentle on yourself and others.

Release judgments and prejudices.

Open up to the courage to examine their grip on your own identity.

We are all one, albeit colorful and diverse expressions of that oneness.

Butterflies are pollinators of transformational seeds of growth into our souls.

Commentary

In the theater of life, the one guaranteed constant is change. The great thing about observing the naturalistic environment of nature is that we see evidence of transience in the changing of the seasons. Think about how crazy it would be to try to rush away winter before the seeds of spring were ready to wake up. The moon doesn't feel resentful of the sun's heat, the sun doesn't get fired up about the moon's control of the tides, and neither does the earth say to the humans that have plundered her resources that we owe her. Do you really think God is egocentric enough to be jealous or vengeful about our behavior? If Jesus, believed by many to be the Son of God, was able to release judgments and forgive his perpetrators while being executed, then surely the Creator was more in touch with his better angels, rather than reacting to the atrocities like the crucifixion without reserve. Meditation on being created in the image of God reveals that, as spiritual beings having human experiences, we understand that we are part creature and part divine. Awakening to the realm of possibilities is about learning how to become free will within the humanity of our actions, rather than be enslaved by a mechanistic worldview of probability and statistics programmed to worship the suffocating ways of materialism. The energy of the butterfly shows us the real possibility of transformation. But transformation goes through stages. What stage of change are you in right now?

Chapter 7

Slithering with Snake in July

This month, we get in touch with our reptilian kin.

We are inspired to shed our old skins!

A full buck moon arrives with the growth of new deer antlers sprouting out of the foreheads of male deer.

As such, we transform the toxicity of venomous snake bites into an alchemy of soulful healing.

Might as well breathe in divine air in the form of crystalline love-light.

Stoking the fire burning within, a passing summer solstice gently nudges us closer to feminine yin.

Meditation on the snake awakens medicinal transformation.

The time is now for heartfelt connections, but don't forget to mind your head.

Disasters leave a crematorium of ashes smoldering underground, igniting new trees to leave underground darkness and branch out into the light.

Pain and suffering are hellish tragedies of life.

Sometimes it's hard not to feel derailed when riding along subways of unwanted emotions.

A sacred marriage between energetic masculine and feminine kin awakens magical rebirths by shedding dead skin.

Commentary

We live in a world full of toxicity. We are constantly being bombarded by lots of energies that leave us feeling depleted. Whether its heavy metals in our bodies, pollution, electromagnetic frequencies, radiation, a shrinking ozone layer, drugs, and so on—there are so many ways to bring us down or perk us up. But in spite of being bitten by these multitudes of venoms, there is so much help waiting to slither in from the spirit realm. All we have to do is ask. Just imagine the possibilities if every one of us started to do this from a clean place in our hearts— without any expectation of getting something in return. It will come about and reflect in our outer world when enough of us shed our old skins and open up to becoming something new. In this way, we will leave behind a clean energetic footprint for others to follow by being a role model. It's like flagging a path for others to follow toward the trail head, to use a hiking metaphor. The trick is to not get stuck in our primitive lizard brain, or reptilian brain. It is easy to become trapped in survival mode—robotic and lost in the everyday busyness of life. But the same systems that oppress can liberate. It is encouraging to know that alternative energy really does start with you. We can all incorporate a meditative way of living by simply becoming mindful of our breathing, picturing calming and peaceful thoughts, expecting synchronicity, and focusing on the positive. Enacting a walking meditation, if you will, really does change our experience with reality and energizes our bodies. This process of transformation is contagious and literally becomes your new normal.

Chapter 8

Dragonfly Lands in August

Dragonfly inspires us to be light on the feet, with magical colors of waning sunlight.

See through illusionary smokescreens through the laser precision eyes of a spiritual watcher.

What hidden aspects of yourself want to come out into the sun and dance in the daylight for others to see?

A full sturgeon moon signals a peak seasonal catch …

Might as well swim with the current instead of pushing against the primordial power of water.

Dragonfly breathes magic and color into the ordinary doings of everyday life.

A long time ago …

Dragon had the Midas touch of always going straight for the gold, but a wise guy called Coyote tricked Dragon by shrinking him down to a fly so that he could eat a slice of humble pie

Do you need a change in habit?

What good are your lucky charms if you get consumed by your own facade?

Let go of the shores, and surrender to life's oceanic bounty.

Are you holding yourself back with programmed beliefs that want to break out of their boxes in mental compartments?

Lighten up by picturing a dragonfly making dazzling aerial feats in the wide open vastness of your infinite inner space …

Ask for directional guidance to see through illusionary smokescreens—allow transformational pathways to become self-evident truths.

Summer is a powerful time to act and create change in your life!

But it won't be long before nature reflects a colorful transition, when autumn leaves behind fleeting energetic balance and fallen old selves.

Life is a mystery. Isn't the destination really the adventure of the journey?

Commentary

August is a mysterious month. It is a time where it feels very much like the heat of summer will last forever. But even early on in the month—if you look carefully—you can see subtle evidence that fall is coming. Perhaps it's a fallen leaf or a hint of color that looks out of place in a tree line of green. Dragonflies are colorful creatures that do incredible feats. They are good reminders that it is a magical, mysterious, and colorful world out there. Use their energies to see through the smoke and mirrors and awaken a more authentic and meaningful life experience. Remember to get out and play outside and meditate on the healing application of water.

Chapter 9

Preparing for a Spirited September Harvest with Squirrel

Squirrel guides us into the realm of getting back to school and down to business ...

While looking at the weather forecast ahead, we are preparing for a winter storage or a time when resources are less plentiful.

Picture sobering up, getting organized, and cross-referencing your planner so that busy fall schedules will not drive you mad.

Squirrels are a good reminder that solid mental health looks like the realization that doing the same thing over and expecting different results—is likely to drive you nuts.

Autumn equinox reminds us of the transitory balance of light and dark energies ... Yin (feminine) and yang (masculine) are dancing together in equal step.

In the Northern Hemisphere, we are moving further into the dark nights of our souls to reach its zenith on the winter solstice in later December.

On the opposite side of the same coin, our friends in the Southern Hemisphere know a similar energetic balance, awakening to a vernal equinox in their spring.

They will see the sunlight expands as darkness contracts, reaching its climax on summer solstice.

At this time, nature reflects a most sweet and satisfying sensual equanimity ... if only fleetingly and transient

Commentary

Fall and spring equinoxes are similar in the sense that masculine and feminine energies are in balance and reflected that way in nature. Given that we are part of nature, these are good times of year to meditate on these energies fluctuating together in natural equality both intrinsically and outwardly. This is an especially good time of year to marvel at the cocreative universal impetus for an egalitarian new world. Of course the building blocks of this new way of living on this earth starts with you! The light of masculine-yang is the opposite side of the same coin as the dark of feminine-yin. We cannot get to the light unless we traverse the dark. Conversely, we cannot know the dark unless we walk in the light. Yang is expressive and outward in its movement. Yin, on the other hand, is receptive and inward in its expression. Those of us in the Northern Hemisphere can stand to realize that our friends in the south are experiencing energetic alignment in much the same way we are, except they will be moving in a masculine-yang-light direction, whereas those of us in the north are moving in a feminine-yin-dark direction. If you prefer the dark and it is the opposite time of year where you live, the good news is that you have something to look forward to. In the meantime, we might as well find a way to accept, appreciate, and even embrace the opposite of our energetic preference.

Chapter 10

Hang Gliding in October with Bat

Bats echo a ring tone of the metaphorical death of the old self, but hang in there, folks …

Like the changing leaves, nature reflects a metamorphosis coming.

Our inner world is ripe for change, especially during these transitional times.

Facing our fears head on is less scary than avoiding situations based only on our fear-based projections.

A full hunter's moon signals that it is time to hunt enough food in remembrance of an old traditional preparation for winter storage.

Do you see the veils falling back?

They are leaving behind the dirge of an old world.

Spirited energies are hanging around our planetary consciousness—bursting at the seams to turn our world around right-side up!

Now is a good time for rebirth by looking at our world with fresh new eyes.

Venture back to your childhood innocence

What unexplored caves of your hidden self are wanting to be discovered today?

What novel solutions are waiting for us to tap into as we move through a purification process of releasing and healing old wounds so that we can give birth to a parallel new age?

Hear the echoes of spirit whispering who we are becoming …

Commentary

Like the seasons, the one constant in life is change. The bat symbolizes this awareness and can help you awaken to understanding that transformation and metamorphosis are real possibilities during your human experience as a spiritual being. Even in stagnation, the power for change is always possible. While our bodies die and we only exist once in this form, it is wise to entertain that our souls have experienced past lives and will rebirth into further lifetimes down the line. But regardless of whether or not you believe in reincarnation, we all journey through many deaths and rebirths in this current life form. You are not the same person now as you were then. And you will not be the same person tomorrow as you are today. Every single snowflake has something uniquely different in its expression, yet all are made mostly of water, just like we are. Water ebbs, flows, and changes its trajectory just like we do. Sometimes personal and collective transformation comes on like a tsunami, and sometimes the process begins as a soliloquy before becoming a grand performance. Perhaps you remember a time in your life where you were just sort of hanging around daydreaming. And then you learned to stand with your feet firmly planted on the ground. But now you have learned to spread your wings and fly in a way that feels like you are hang gliding through life.

Chapter 11

November Roosts in with Turkey

Turkey guides us into the shared space of gratitude and infinite blessings.

Even if they are notorious for stealing from their fellow nervous woodland creature, squirrel friends have winter stockpiles of food storage ...

In this way, nature hold up a mirror to look at the power of leveling impulses.

Let us give back to our Mother Earth as a way of saying thank you for the abundance she has provided us.

Picture a turkey to ward off any negative energies that might be sucking on your energy field and leaving you feeling drained.

A full beaver moon reminds us of a time when peak beaver activity inspired our ancestors to set traps before swamps froze.

We all need enough fur to keep our bodies warm to survive the cold winter months.

In that industry, turkey helps our souls warm up to the idea of feeding ourselves a clean spiritual diet.

We are waking up to the birth of a new age and paradigm, lifting the veil from our third eye that has been sleeping in a hypnotic trance for a long time.

A critical mass of feminine energy is gaining power in numbers.

Trying to put the brakes on this yin-bound train will only delay our gratification, met with predictive futile resistance.

Equal access to resources is an unfolding convergence of harmony again of sustainable living for our planetary consciousness and beyond.

Commentary

Imagine all of us sharing our resources and gaining equal access to the greater good. We know that we have been well trained to divide and conquer and view ourselves as separate from one another. In that, we have become good at making judgments about each other as being either superior or inferior by sizing one another up. But in today's tumultuous times, we have been given a clear view of perspective taking. A culture of egalitarianism is being born, albeit not without labor pains. While the pain is inevitable, suffering is a choice. The freedom to choose whether or not we will continue to suffer is a powerful choice. Waking up to finding a way out of the suffering is in our best interest as a collective consciousness. Abundance is a real possibility. We will know when a critical mass is here when enough of us choose to believe it and see the change reflected in a new world revealed before our eyes.

Chapter 12

Rising to the Summit with Mountain Lion in December

In a world full of loud leaders pounding their chests to be seen and heard, mountain lion embodies a gentle roar quietly leading by example.

But in authentic feline fashion, your leadership will probably go unnoticed by many.

Know that your personal power makes you a cool cat commanding the call of respect.

A full cold moon signifies the coldest, darkest, and longest nights of the year—especially on the winter solstice, where the dark night of feminine-yin energy reaches her energetic peak.

Following that, we start coaxing back the light as the days slowly become longer as the sunlight of masculine-yang energy gains momentum.

On the opposite side of the same coin, our friends in the Southern Hemisphere experience peak light as masculine-yang reaching its zenith on the summer solstice.

Now their days will slowly become shorter as movement into the dark grows in power.

True power builds gradually like water, but the attached price tag of responsibility need not make you hiss.

Mountain lion is king of playing situational football at its finest.

Know in your personal authority that you have the ability to effectively adjust your game plan at any given moment and respond accordingly.

Do you remember the power of our tribal African shamanic brothers and sisters?

Fly away and meditate on the elemental forces of water and darkness for a spell …

How many times have we feared our own primal, dark, and feminine nature?

The power of the internal martial arts is cultivated gradually.

A cumulative effect of simmering softness of feminine energy has risen again.

Commentary

In our modern world, we often think of power as a position of leadership that basks in the limelight. We often look for those in positions of leadership to the answers and solve our problems. Yes, we do need movers and shakers to share access to resources and do their part with the right intention. But we all have a natural humble leader on the inside. Like an ocean bowing to the rivers that flow into it, the energy of the mountain lion is a quiet yet powerful spirit guide to tap into. In terms of a popular leader, the Dalai Lama symbolizes this kind of power. He represents the wave of the future when it comes to an embodiment of egoless power and a good role model. This is the kind of power, though radical humility, that you can relax into by just knowing that it is there for you and society to share. But don't go looking for awards, accolades, or special recognition, because this kind of cat is working in hidden, shadowy caverns and crevasses more than out in broad daylight.

Conclusion

It is my hope that this book will feel like a breath of fresh air in the present moment of your life today. I have a prayerful and meditative dream that we will all know inner peace and witness its reflection on planet earth and the greater collective universe. The time is now, brothers and sisters. We are all needed to move forward in our evolution as spiritual beings having human and otherwise experiences. Nature loves us when we take a moment to appreciate and show gratitude to her bounty. She gives us an unlimited abundance of sunlight, dark nights, wind, rain, dead calm, and storm fronts and a generalized sense of unpredictability. Sometimes nature comes to you in the form of a rainbow, just when you were feeling lost and alone. But don't let this drive you mad. The polarity of a full moon and a starry night, juxtaposed with a dark moon on a black night, give us a point of reference. Without the cold wind blowing deep into the dark chambers of our souls, we would not know the pure joy of a fun on a sunny day. And we wouldn't have something else to complain about, which is a popular and repetitive topic these days. All you have to do is look beneath the headlines, and you will see the world is at it is. It does not need to be saved or fixed. Rather, nature will heal itself as we heal ourselves so that we are harmonizing with our natural environment. This world needs characters. Without that friend with a flat affect or depleted air or sour grapes vibe, there wouldn't be that friend who is happy-go-lucky, bubbly, or generally magically sociable and upbeat. Without the stoic personalities and odd ducks, there would be no animation in our fellowship with one another. May we cultivate tolerance and acceptance and even learn to embrace one another in our totality. Surrender, let go, and release your old wounds to be recycled into the light. Become wholeness. We got this. Everybody, do this.

Printed in the United States
By Bookmasters